Journeys

THROUGH INNER SPACE

PAINTINGS & POEMS BY HUE WALKER

POMEGRANATE ARTBOOKS ✳ SAN FRANCISCO

This work is dedicated to the recovery of our Mother Earth

Front cover: *Immram*
Back cover: *Green Awakening*

All of the paintings in this book are acrylic on paper and measure 15 x 11 inches (or 11 x 15 inches) except *Gaia Crucified*, which is 7 x 5 inches, and *Wolf Song*, which is 19 x 24 inches.

Published by Pomegranate Artbooks
Box 6099, Rohnert Park, California 94927

Library of Congress Cataloging-in-Publication Data

Walker, Hue.
      Journeys through inner space : paintings & poems / by Hue Walker. — 1st ed.
          p.   cm.
      ISBN 0-87654-474-X
      1. Walker, Hue —Themes, motives.   I. Title.
   NX512.W35A4   1995
   759.13—dc20   95-30726
                                                               CIP

Pomegranate catalog no. A802

Designed by Tim Lewis

Printed in Korea
00 99 98 97 96 95 6 5 4 3 2 1

First Edition

CONTENTS

Poems and Paintings

ACKNOWLEDGMENTS

I wish to acknowledge and to thank all who have added a spice or a stir to my cauldron, but especially the following:

my mother, Betty, and my grandmother Mary for teaching me to appreciate the spirit;

Carol, who was the first to suggest a book;

Grace and Catharine, who first taught me the value of questions;

all the members of our ritual circle for their wonderful humor;

my full moon sisters, Erin, Mary, and Jo, for long, nutritious conversations;

Pat, for allowing my muse to ride her brush when my brush must be at rest;

Dane, for stretching my boundaries;

Sam, whose glowing praise feeds my muse;

Mary Elkins, for her superb photography and willingness to share her expertise;

John, who helped me give form to my journeys;

all the writers and painters and musicians who have stirred my soup, especially Joy Harjo and Wendell Berry, Botticelli and Vincent;

Meinrad, for nurturing my world of symbols;

my dog, Sophy, for her patience;

the extraordinary beech trees at Avebury;

Tom and Katie Burke of Pomegranate for their generous support and encouragement;

Robert, whose enthusiasm gave me the courage to take this project seriously;

and most especially my daughter, Quinn, for keeping me honest, and my husband, Bradley, my traveling companion, for his frequent reassurances that my time has been well spent.

—H.W.

INTRODUCTION

BY ROBERT LENTZ

This is, indeed, the best of times and yet the worst of times. Human history and the world as we have known it both hang on a slender thread above destruction. Dominant groups within our race have pushed us to this point by failing to keep knowledge and wisdom in balance. But the peril now confronting us is also breaking the spell under which we have labored blindly for so many centuries, enabling us to choose a radically different path for the future. This choice is the slender thread upon which we hang, and it is the theme of this collection of Hue Walker's poetic essays and haunting visual images.

Natural catastrophes and hostile invasions by other human groups have brought an end to many of our cultures and civilizations in the past, but no culture or civilization has long survived its neglect of wisdom. Both knowledge and wisdom are essential to human life. Knowledge acquaints us with our physical surroundings and enables us to sustain our lives. Wisdom enables us to judge what use we will make of the knowledge we acquire. Both engage our intellect, but wisdom arises from our heart and soul—and reposes therein.

*   *   *   *   *

I live along the Rio Grande, a rich bottomland with millions of years of alluvial sediment brought down from the mountains to the north. Plant life abounds here, ranging from majestic cottonwoods to a multitude of grasses and wildflowers. Coyotes, hawks, beavers, roadrunners, and countless other animals do their daily dance in and around the river. Mountains many thousands of feet high loom in the distance on every side, and the starkly beautiful desert begins as the land rises from the river.

For three hundred years Hispanic Catholics have tilled this valley and blessed it with their processions and prayers. Their homes and mine sit on the ruins of sixteen pre-Columbian villages. Pot shards work their way to the earth's surface now and then, reminding us of the past. On volcanic cliffs to the west, petroglyphs speak of a more ancient worldview, in which balance with nature and the goodness of the earth were so important.

In this same valley, not far from my home, there is an evangelical Christian center with a large wooden gate bearing inscriptions on both sides. On the inside, but still visible from the road, the gate proclaims, "You are now entering a lost and dying world." The gate stands in direct opposition to reality as it has been *experienced* here for thousands of years. It leads through an adobe wall six feet high, which shuts out the valley and any world larger than that defined by the evangelicals. I shudder whenever I pass that place, for it epitomizes for me the spell that has blinded us for so long.

Every culture has had its creation myth that has laid its metaphysical foundations for daily life. Most myths were never written down before the arrival of anthropologists. They were simply repeated on winter nights from one generation to the next. They included accounts of the first people—and very often a first father and mother—and how the primal ancestors found their way to the sacred center of creation, making mistakes along the way, but always learning from those mistakes.

The evangelicals here have such a myth, a myth they share with their Catholic neighbors but which they emphasize in different ways. It was written down thousands of years ago and then rewritten several times, until it has become a confusing patchwork quilt of contradictory themes. Unlike myths of most other cultures, it has claimed to be the only true version of how things began. Wherever its followers have carried it, they have suppressed other myths with either ridicule or flame. As a result, it has become one of the major metaphysical underpinnings for late twentieth-century Earth and the origin of the terrible imbalance that has brought us to the brink of self-destruction. Even people who reject this myth are influenced by the forces and institutions it legitimatizes.

The myth is found in Genesis, and with its many revisions, it reflects much of the suffering in Western history. The roots of this myth come from ancient Mesopotamia, but they were drastically edited centuries later by Hebrew warrior-priests bent on establishing hierarchies of power. The editing was so thorough that the end result now stands in direct opposition to the ancient myths.

The hierarchies of power that the warrior-priests established begin with the earth itself, which is given to human beings to fill and *conquer*. Then humankind is split along gender lines, and men are placed above women. Finally, through the paradigm of disobedience and the fall, humans—even males—are subtly told to discredit their own judgment and submit to religious authority. The way is paved for intricate codes of law and enforcement. The chosen are blessed to conquer not only infidels, but even the planet which sustains them.

Western history is filled with dangerous memories that have been suppressed beneath official versions of how things have come to be. One of these suppressed memories is that millions of Europeans lost their lives as Christian orthodoxy was forced on the continent's many populations. What began somewhat peacefully and resulted in a mixture of Christian and pre-Christian beliefs was later turned into a literal holocaust with the appearance of the Inquisition. Added to these millions in Europe are additional millions in North and South America and other parts of the world who lost their lives as Christian culture—and the myth of Genesis—advanced behind the sword. In this way, a self-destructive version of the ancient Middle Eastern myths came to displace traditional wisdom in cultures far from its source and to dominate human thought and behavior throughout the world.

The myth of Genesis has brought us to the brink of destruction because it has placed our species in an adversarial position with our planet. It has removed us from our legitimate place within creation and placed us above everything else. We are told to conquer the earth, to bring it under our domination and control. We are told to be fertile and to fill the earth with our species—something we have now done, at the expense of countless other species of plants and animals, whose presence, we now realize, helped sustain our own.

Modern science is the child of western Europe and grew to what it has now become with the blessings spoken in Genesis. It has brought technological advances in both health and the production of wealth to many parts of the Western world. The West nurtures such hope in its science that this in itself has become an extension of the Genesis myth, even replacing Genesis for the vast portions of the Western world that are now estranged from Judaism or Christianity. No problem is too great for science to overcome; that is, every aspect of the earth can be conquered in the end, so that the survival of the human race may be assured. The myth so thoroughly edited by the ancient warrior-priests and meant to support the religious institutions they valued has thus come full circle and replaced their religion, by making humankind supreme in itself. The continuing growth of this myth fills the pages and frames of our science fiction novels and films.

While Genesis remains a myth and continues to have its deepest influence on the Western psyche as a myth, it has not been treated as a myth by the powers it has legitimatized. This, in fact, is a major part of the problems stemming from Genesis. The higher the edifice one hopes to build, the more substantial the foundation one must place beneath it; and when one claims that one's species owns a planet, or that one's gender is superior to the other, or that one's religion is the only *true* religion in the world, or that one's ethnic group is divinely chosen from all others, or that one's religious leader is infallible, then it is especially important to have an unshakable base for such unlikely claims. Judeo-Christian scriptures, containing the myths that have shaped the Western psyche, are claimed to be divinely inspired in a way that surpasses claims made by any other religious groups, save Islam. Biblical myths have been removed from the realm of ordinary mythology and have been forced to serve instead as history. This is fundamentalism, and biblical fundamentalism is as old as the ancient Hebrew warrior-priests who gave Genesis its final form.

Biblical myths have been turned into a weapon to defend the powers that depend upon them, and with the attempted suppression of all competing myths, this has meant the imposition of *one* way of seeing reality. This one way favors left-brain thought, the validation of force to overcome obstacles, the exaltation of heterosexual males above all other humans, and the sense that the earth is a hostile, dark force—the "lost and dying world" of the New Mexican evangelicals—which must be brought under human control.

Because this interpretation was originally based on claims of divine origin, it has been considered unquestionable until recently. Even people who no longer consider the Bible to be inerrant cling to what the Bible has created, without questioning their reasons. This view of reality has justified the murder of millions of persons who have stood in its way, be they pagans, heretics, or even coreligionists who simply lived on the wrong side of a political boundary. It has blessed the growth of capitalism, the wasteful exploitation of the earth's limited resources, the development of ever more destructive weapons of war, and even the destruction of the very ecosystems that sustain human life. Faced with the real possibility of nuclear warfare or the equally fatal possibility of contamination by nuclear waste; faced with overpopulation and the daily starvation of thousands of human beings; faced with global warming, the increased incidence of skin cancer because of the vanishing ozone layer in our atmosphere, and chemical pollution of the air, water, and food that sustain our lives; we have reached the point where we can and must admit that the emperor isn't wearing any clothes.

As we hang from our slender thread, the way out of this peril is to find other ways to interpret reality. We have been infatuated for centuries with knowledge and the power it has brought us to dominate and control the earth and one another. Before the thread snaps we must rediscover wisdom, which comes only from long and profound experience of life. Because the thread is so thin and the weight we have accumulated so great, there would be little hope of survival if we were left to our own resources. Fortunately, however ruthlessly the forces of orthodoxy advanced, they failed to destroy everything in their path. We can still find traces of ancient wisdom at the periphery of our world and, building on these, can come much sooner to a wisdom of our own.

The impact of Judeo-Christian orthodoxy on the Western world has been like a stone thrown into a pond. It has been strongest at the center, with concentric ripples becoming increasingly fainter as they have moved toward the edge. Both in Europe and the Americas, Christianity's impact was most disruptive in the centers of population, but rural populations were left more to their own, except in the times of the worst persecutions. The word "pagan" itself originally simply referred to a country dweller, and since country dwellers tended to retain more of the ancient wisdom and beliefs of their forebears, "pagan" eventually came to mean "non-Christian." Today this form of Christianity that survived at the edges of power is called "folk Catholicism." It has little parallel among Protestant groups, since the essence of Protestantism has been to root out anything that was not biblical.

Folk Catholicism still thrives in rural areas of Europe and in most of Latin America. There we can find traces of time-tried wisdom from pre-Christian cultures, buried beneath Judeo-Christian forms. Some of that healthy paganism exists among my Hispanic neighbors, and it is partly against this that the evangelicals have built their symbolic six-foot adobe wall. Mystics within Judaism and Christianity have also managed to retain wisdom, however surrounded they may have been by the lust for power, simply because their knowledge of the divine has come from their own experience in the world and not merely from official religious teachings. We can therefore turn to the mystics of Europe as well for the wisdom we so desperately need in our day. It is ironic that these mystics and the vast peasant populations have both been seen by the forces at the center as a threat to Christianity and Judaism, since they are all that tie these otherwise self-destructive systems to life-giving wisdom.

Another source to which we can turn are the non-Christian cultures of the Third World and those cultures that archaeology is bringing back to light from the past. There we will find wisdom garnered from millennia of lived experience that will teach us how to rejoin the rest of creation instead of continuing to pit ourselves against it. Many times these cultures will not present us with a written literature, so we will have to listen instead to their stories and silently gaze at their visual art or their expressive rituals. This in itself will be healthful for us who are so often trapped in the left side of our brains.

Put the simplest way possible, our survival depends on whether we can recognize that we have been careening the wrong way down a one-way street, that we have defined as "forward" what has actually been "backward," and that we need to make a 180-degree turn as quickly as possible. Whatever great contributions our scientists and theoreticians have made to the quality of our lives, if those lives are to continue much longer, we now need once again the shaman and the mystic. Our supposed sophistication has in fact been a form of anorexia. We will not survive without this earth, and we must turn now to the earth and to those who live close to the earth to learn how to survive.

I first met Hue Walker on a cold winter solstice night in 1991. She and her family joined my friends and me as we danced outside around a blazing Yule bonfire and retold Celtic myths from millennia past. Since then we have leapt many a ceremonial bonfire together at the turnings of the year and have sat over many a cup of wine, discussing life and wisdom we have rediscovered from sources far and wide. I have watched with fascination as she has produced one luminous painting after another, weaving together so many strands of wisdom from different cultures, a veritable Spider Woman for our own times. These paintings are beacons as we search for a path into the future. In some ways I have felt myself a midwife to this book, so it is with the pride and joy of one who has assisted at its birth that I introduce it to the world.

STATEMENT OF...

The Usual phrase is,
    "Statement of Purpose."
Many projects are begun with a
    "Statement of Purpose."

But I am ending here,
This last string of words,
    written after all the images
    have found their way out.
These words come
    to try and frame the work,
To try and give a sense
    of what I think I might
        have been about
        these last three years.

But the point is,
    I have only clues,
    bits and pieces.

These images came
    only after I was able
    to just let them be.
To allow them to come into existence
    without full explanation.
To allow my hands to paint the images
    just as they flowed out
    without thinking them into
    a logical and sensible death.
Without allowing my intellect to
    orchestrate, officiate, direct
        a stillbirth.

And so, I have only clues.
    I know this is about
        the Planet,
        and Us.
        And what "Us" means.

I know this is about
            walking in beauty.

    And about Respect.

    It's about questioning
            Strongly held values.
    Throwing out
            Strongly held values.
    And looking for
            Simple Respect,
            Humble Respect.
                    Reverence.

I put forward these images from my hands,
    with this prayer:

    May all of my human sisters and brothers
            be one day able
            to look around at all of creation,
            be able to look at wolves and deer,
            sequoias and oaks, rivers and sky,
    And see brothers and sisters.
    Be able to look at beetles and seagulls,
            and dandelions and dirt,
    And feel the family tie.

Because we are not capable of justice
    within our human family,
As long as we hold ourselves separate.

As long as we are capable of wanton destruction,
    We will inevitably aim it
            at our own kind as well.

– H.W.

Durham Cathedral

I went on the long journey
    to stand in those sacred places.
I gathered my family and my savings,
    studied maps and books,
And we took the long journey.
We spent a summer turning paper photos
    into experience of place.

I wanted to see standing stones
    and Great Art.

I wanted to stand in places where
    my kind had been working the riddles
    long enough to become the riddle.

We traveled the steel arteries
    of the Old World
    examining the riddle.

And one place where antiquity,
    standing stone, and
        Great Art
    promised to cross paths,
Was at Durham Cathedral.

And when I came home and began
    To Paint,
    To finally allow the river of images
    To flow through,
The imagery began with this archway.
    These stones cut so long ago,
    That the elements have almost
        settled the question of
        what is the true form of stone?
All those hours spent carving and measuring
    washing back into the river
    one grain at a time.

And I remember the experience
    of that place.
    Where light and air and sky
        are shut out by
        the pride of accomplishment.

Somehow this was a monument not to
　　The Creator,
　　but to the creators themselves.
　　The town fathers competing,
　　as men do,
　　for the tallest tower.

These stones support,
　　wondrous stone vaulting.
　　It really is incredible to see.
The cathedrals are astonishing monuments
　　to the cleverness of my kind.
But that's really all I found there.
Cleverness outshines the sacred
　　in the cathedrals.

But then, the weight of Avebury's stones
　　speaks of pride in cleverness, too.

But at least the vault they support
　　still carries the stars,
　　and allows the seeker
　　to look past the stone
　　and into the mystery.

Maybe that's why the men of Durham
　　had to shut out the sky?
　　To cut down on the distractions.
Mystery and Riddle are very distracting.

Maybe that's why the Great Clever Ones
　　have always disdained
　　the country folk,
　　the "heathens,"
　　the "pagans,"
　　the "rubes,"
Because those close to the soil
　　are too involved in
　　living the mysteries
　　to be a good audience.

DURHAM CATHEDRAL

THE INNER DOORWAY

This is my house,
  My flesh,
  Swept clean of
  The clutter of living.

I leave the followers of The One Way
    to their carefully described pathways.

And I open the windows
    to the night air.

Drawing on the wisdom of the old ones,
  I bless the doorway
  and step through,
To play among the riddles.

THE INNER DOORWAY

GAVRINIS

Gavrinis, in Brittany,
I have expended immense energies
    to stand in this place,
    and to touch these stones
    and to be present in this mystery.

And in this place I the painter feel
    an intense resonance
    with the visionary,
        the old one,
        who thought of this place
        and then made it be.

And having reached this place
    and wandered this mystery
I paint these stones
        as Labyrinth,
    with many and varied ways,
        each pathway leading
        to the center
        to find waiting
        a question.

GAVRINIS

HAND AXE

It is the way of the hand
        to make changes.
The object idly held
       and toyed with
or purposefully grasped
       and manipulated

Becomes other.
    The rounded river pebble
       becomes a hand axe,
       becomes a beautiful object of
      Change.

And in each change
   another doorway opens.
      The path forks
And the questions intensify.

And Coyote follows after us
   Just to see
      what we have done.

HAND AXE

WINTER SOLSTICE

The Year turns toward the darkness,
    toward the still time
    for contemplation and rest.

The cold nights have a clarity,
    which draws me out under the stars,
    to breathe in the ice-crystaled air,
    and look out into the deep ocean of the cosmos.

The deepest mystery lies here.
    The mystery of human and divine
        and creature and soul,
    Of death and rebirth
        and circular existence.

The living flame cradled in the brown paper
    has an eloquence
    unavailable
    to the great cathedral.

This is one of the places where the old ones
    can commune with
    the mystery which the cathedrals
    have failed to contain.

WINTER SOLSTICE

WOLF SONG

They are too like us.
They look at us with such
       Knowledge
   of us, looking
    straight through us.
We cannot hide from them.

Perhaps that explains the strychnine,
   and the steel traps,
Because they eat from the same plate.

And yet these, our closest fur companions,
   look at our pathways
   in such puzzlement.

They will gladly take up our fraying threads
   and reweave us with the moon
   if we will only listen
     to the singing.

WOLF SONG

GAIA CRUCIFIED

Connectedness.

We are all connected.
    Each two-legged, six-legged,
        furry, scaly, leafy, twiggy,
        mineral or elemental being,
    Is a piece of the whole,
        of which I am a part.

I Am Creation.

And the sins which
    are destroying our Home,
        our Mother

Can only be committed
        by severed beings,
    Those who have ripped out
        their own bleeding roots,
And strike out from
    the agony of isolation.

GAIA CRUCIFIED

IMBOLC

Early spring
    when the lambs are born
    and the milk flows
    and the farmer's cycle
    is at its most beginning place.

The fields glow with
    possibility,
    with the mystery.

At the other end of the year
    the crow dances on the stubble.
New life implies
    the end of life.

And at the crossing point
    Brigid's flame dances,
    The spark of inspiration
        which must burn the brighter
        in recognition of darkness.

KOKOPELI AND THE GODDESS

A little Neolithic Goddess, White Clay,
Tumbled in the Timestream.
So beautiful, So sensuous, full, fertile,
      Her form calling up
           Grandma hugs & cotton aprons & bread dough
              & babies & lovers
        & the fullness of a life lived in place
              in the arms of the Mother.

But She's been tumbled in Time,
    Rolled down the Patriarchal Centuries.
And in her long journey she has been diminished
      her hands
      her feet
      her head
      broken off and lost in the civilizing.
The Timestream tried to wear her smooth and round
              and unrecognizable.
But she started out smooth and round and
          Whole
      and now she is broken and jagged.

But her heart remains,
      and her womb,
      and we can recognize Her familiar beauty still.
She is not lost,
      only bound.

And Kokopeli, the flute player, the bent one,
            the seed-bringer,
Still lurks in the best of men.
And He calls to Her
And offers Her Music & Dance & Love,
    and bids Her be Whole and Wholly Alive again.

CERNUNNOS SLEEPS

The Old God sleeps
    down in the dark, moist,
        odorous underfoot,

Waiting for us
    to put down our roots.

CERNUNNOS SLEEPS

THE GREEN MAN SLEEPS

The Green Man lies beneath the ground
    having given himself in faith
    to the Sacred Riddle.

Life Springs from Death.

The May King must die to give life to
    the land.

The tree stands naked to winter storm,
    having given her cloak of leaves
    into the transformative keeping
        of the Mother.

The winter stillness,
    that breath-holding moment,
    after the act of faith,
    and before the hoped-for spring,
When the gift of fear,
    warms the heart which sleeps beneath the snow.

THE GREEN MAN SLEEPS

GREEN AWAKENING

Life,
So vibrant, Bursting forth,
    and varied beyond imagining,
And so delicate, so fragile.

We bruise Her so easily,
Yet Gaia clings to her little ones
    with such tenacity!

The Dance between The Beings,
    born with
        the Collective Unconscious,
Demands space for the steps,
    Insists we listen to the Beat!

The Mother, Mammau, She gives birth,
    She gives birth, She gives birth,
        She gives birth.

The Son, the Father, the Hunter, the Hunted,
    the Horned One, the "Jack'i'th'Green,"
        The Very, Quivering, Odorous "I AM!"
            beneath the forest floor,
    Rises up to meet Her.

ENFOLDING MYSTERY

She is the Quiet One,
　　The Waiting One.
She who sits and spins,
　　and waits for her tired little ones
　　to climb back into her lap to rest.

She sings the Great Note of Beginning,
　　and waits to fold her cloak of shadow
　　　　around those who venture
　　　　　　out into her vast sea
　　　　　　　　of mystery.

She sets all to spinning,
　　combs the fibers into order,
　　and holds the secrets of
　　navigating the tangles.

She is the Great Shadow inherent in
　　All Light.

She sits among the tangled roots of existence
　　　　Silent Singing,
　　　　Presence Itself.

ENFOLDING MYSTERY

CORN MOTHER

The Living Earth,
　　Mineral Being,
　　Breathes Her force upward
　　　　and carries the miracle
　　　　　　within the seeds
　　Outward into the Cosmos.

And the planetary bodies
　　dance circles within circles
　　while the women's hands
　　pat out today's bread.

The water flows
　　around the edges of
　　　　this place,
　　Here.
And She listens, savoring,
　　as the great serpent
　　　　sings to Her of
　　　　　　danger,
　　　　　　　and the edge of being.

CORN MOTHER

DREAM VISION

I stand in the crossing
    of a damp-plaster-smelling church.
Mother guards the doorway
    blocking the exit with
    little bricks of fear.
Her mother hovers in the vaulting,
    clutching silvered crystal rosaries
    and sweat-stained scapulars.

The art is all gone, leaving only
    carelessly matched patches.

The labyrinth presents but one way,
    clever beauty,
    but only one way,
    the goal visible and unchanging.

I stand at the crossing
    of this hollow building,
    And I see for the first time
        the southern door stands open.

The corner for fire, and passion, and inspiration.
    South, sun side, high Noon.

The door stands open.
    I follow the light, straight across
        the twisted singular way
        and out onto the earth.

My feet touch the grass,
    And my eyes touch
    the pure light
    promising vision.

DREAM VISION

ANASAZI GATEWAY

The great kiva at Chaco.

The shovels of the rational ones
    scrape off the earth
    looking for answers.
They find only questions.

This great kiva once held secrets.
    Now open to the cosmos,
        it seems . . .
    One of those border places.
        At once stripped stark,
            vastly empty,
        Yet entirely filled,
            having been opened up
            to contain all the secrets.

This is one of those border-places
    where The Mystery takes a stand,
    and defies the rational ones.
    A place where the many
        find, each, their own.

This is a place where Gaia opens up
    and invites her thinkers
        to look at what we have done.

ANASAZI GATEWAY

NIGHT WINGS

The raven glides on feathered darkness.
    One of the boundary dwellers.
A shard of night challenging sunlight,
    conceding only slivers of oily color.

Mystery dwells in the borderlands,
    eluding rational explanation,
    and the cries of, "Demon!"
Dancing outside the walls built of hurled bricks,
Inviting the wakeful ones to venture out.

The Sword of Righteousness Divides,
    only divides,
    Everything,
        into good and evil,
        into dark and light,
        into We and They.
    Carving away and discarding
        exactly one half
        of Creation.

The beginning of wholeness requires
    only unknowing.

NIGHT WINGS

EYES OF DREAMTIME

Dream.
The refuge of symbol
    in a rational world.
Where clay babies live for days
    in the forgotten dust,
    then, suckled, stir,
    and run on puppy legs.
Where shapechange can still exist,
    unquestioned,
    outside of scientific orthodoxy.

River cascade of hair flows unexplained
    between mud bank hands,
    and quill pen dips in vein ink.

Dream spills into waking
    and we walk the path of symbol and image
    Seeing through Other-eyes
    the cosmos within.

Some walk straight in rational shoes,
    and leave the dreaming for the sleepers.
Yet the dreamtime stalks the waking world,
    leaving changelings.

SACRED MADNESS

Mad Sweeney walks the shaman's path,
    medieval Irish face
    of a tale with countless lives.

The tale of the one who crosses over.
    One who can no longer lie and deny.
    One to whom truth has become
        the only way.

Some seek that path through vision quest,
    through study, trial, and contemplation.
    Some turn blind eyes to the open doorway.

Some are born with their feet on the path,
    or find themselves engulfed in vision,
    The shelter of denial forever lost,
Pursued along each path
    by the ancient face of wisdom,
    by the enigma of death dealing birth.

Personal boundaries shift and fade,
    merge with the feathered beings.
The world of human contempt for other life forms,
    ceases to exist,
    For the shape shifters.
For those who willingly bear
    the burden of wisdom.

SACRED MADNESS

CIRCLE SONG

Mystery
  Some say hoax. Some say UFOs,
  Wind vortices, Military experiments.
  Electro-magnetic disturbances.
  What bends the grain down?

But maybe it's pulled down from below,
  Not pushed over, but summoned down,
    to lie along the Mother,
  To form a pattern which says . . .
  What? . . .
  Something . . .
  Some message, no one can agree.

But the important thing is,
  We are talking about it,
  And wondering about it,
  And longing collectively for mystery,
  Somehow disappointed by mundane explanations or confessions,
  Needing to be baffled, and puzzled and teased.

And regardless of why the grain bows over,
  the point is to take off our shoes
  and listen through the souls of our feet
  to The Beat!

CIRCLE SONG

BOUNDARIES

In Celtic Mythology
This world and the Otherworld
   lie alongside each other
       nested together
   like the layers of driftwood
     or of a seashell,
Their boundaries shifting and permeable,
   The crossings simple acts for Gods and birds
   and mythical adventures for humankind.

We guard these entryways with charm and ritual
   And shiver at their mention,
       whether in fear or in longing.

The worlds are stitched together at the edges,
Dawn, dusk, the first day of winter,
   or summer,
   or of a life,
The edge of the sea, the riverbank,
   the horizon,
   the mouth of a cave,
   or of a grave.
The stitches held by charm and talisman,
   and words of power.

And the Borderland of human boundaries . . .
   More familiar,
      yet infinitely more mysterious.
The simple boundary of personal space,
The edge of "I" and "other,"
   constantly shifting
   in size and shape and intensity.

The border of sound and music,
   word and poetry,
   utility and beauty.

And there is something delightful,
   and cherished,
   and divine,
In the human heart,
   which takes the bone from
      a dead bird,
   and shapes it into a flute,
   and breathes into it,
   and creates
   a bird's song!

And in this sacred act
   knows all there is to know
   of crossing boundaries.

59

WISDOM

Inspiration dances
　　on the point of a spear,
　　Where flesh and spirit separate.

I reach into the boiling cauldron
　　of Celtic Myth,
　　Into tales of Otherwordly Springs,
　　　　In which swim wisdom imparting salmon
　　　　fed on the fruits
　　　　of otherworldly trees.

I reach into my own dreams and visions
　　of otherwordly teachers
　　and shapeshifting adventure.

And I take the colored threads
　　and weave the myth,
　　As it lives in this time,
　　in this place,
　　in this flesh and spirit.
Allow the current to flow
　　between the banks that I am.

WISDOM

ROOTS

Infinity slices dawn
    And roots reach out into deep space
        into eternity
        into the mystery.
I open my eyes from a forgotten dream
    and before I see the ivied rosy curtains
        I see the Roots,
    For less than a heartbeat
        less than a thoughtbeat
          I see the Roots.

Most roots lie
        Twisted and concealed
        Defying vision
        Defying search
        Teasing understanding
        Mangled by examining spade.
    Yet these roots flash
        in Stark Revelation.
And they remain in my inner gallery of images,
        engraved on the backs of my eyes,
    Waiting not patiently for the brush and colors.

I close my eyes and look into that deep eternity.
I trust my guardians to tether me
        as I lean into the gap
    And venture out on jeweled wings
        into the deep of mystery,
    Vastness beyond familiarity.
    I am a being of wings & fear & trust.

I float at the ends of my spidery threads
        And pray for images.

And I see, obliquely, a point of light,
    Writhing flames of male energy,
        terrible, lightless centered.
A deep breath, feel the tethering threads,
    I turn toward the flare and see
        only pure, flaming male energy
    the lightless center is gone,
        my own fear,
        gone with the direct gaze.

Then I see a vast misty form,
    flowing, transparent female energy
        with seraphic wings,
    steady, outside of time.

The roots are straining toward
        the oldest, faceless, nameless SHE.

And as I watch, the flame enters
    Her womb
    And Her heart
And they are complete
    the One and Oldest Beginning.

ROOTS

65

LORD OF THE LEAST

The Guardian stands
    at the center of the grove.

At once he is
    the strength of oak,
    the fleeting stag
And the Horned One.

And nestled in his bowery cloak
    the jewel-beings,
        flash of delight
        beneath a leaf.

And within his cloak
    clasped in the
        entwining roots,
the entire Cosmos.

The shaman runs
    with the deer,
And boundaries of time
    and place and size and
        being
    blur with the speed of
        motion.

LORD OF THE LEAST

CENTER OAK

Each wanderer moves
    in a mist of symbols,
    surrounded by shards of meaning,
The path behind
    constructed of conclusions,
The path ahead
    of congealing contemplation.

There are moments of clarity,
    etched in colored lines
    on the inner surface
    of the skull.
Images upon which to hang
    the flesh of experience
    and dreaming.

And each one must choose
    to live a life of laps
    on the solid highway of conclusion,
Or to step out onto
    the thin bridge of contemplation.

To drive the shimmering veils of vision
    into the night world of dreaming,
    the last, persistent refuge of symbol,
Or to step fully conscious
    into the Otherworld.

Slip into the bark-skin,
    reach into the soil
    and, with wandering, myriad rootlets,
    search the nether places.
Allow the consciousness to rise with the sap
    along the skyward branchings
    into the scant and icy regions
    above the tallest peaks.

Choose whether to drive out
    the Demons of Unknowing,
Or to revere and celebrate
    Wildness and Mystery.

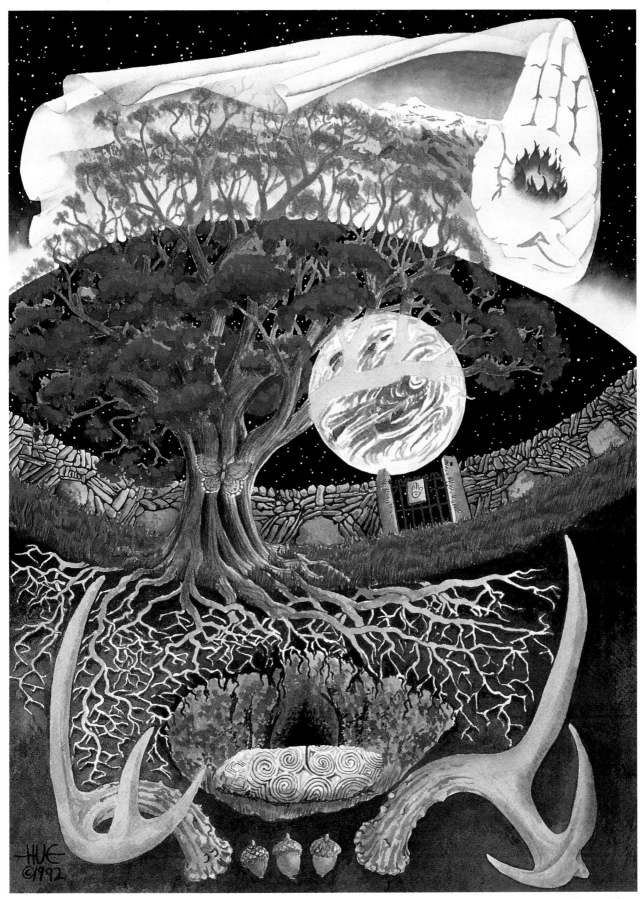

CENTER OAK

TRANSITIONS

Today I walk through a doorway,
An opening into another place,
A place where I am no longer
               the birthgiver
               the child carrier.
This little bit of flesh,
        so powerful,
        so wondrous,
Served me well, served my daughter well,
Provided her doorway into this place,
Kept the river flowing.
Now she is the lock-keeper.
She decides who passes down
        This ancient river.
And now my cavern of flesh
        will be gone into smoke,
        will trouble me no longer.
And I will turn into the
        Cave of Spirit
        Where my vital me
               enters into the new branch
               of the river.
        I will walk this new river bank,
        I will explore the Caverns of Myth
               and allow the great
                       Underworld River
        to flow through my brushes
        and wash the vision onto
               the paper,
Out into the larger family.

71

GUARDIANS

I stand at the center,
    with the morning sun
        on my face,
    And the evening twilight
        at my back.

Cold winds demand
    the attention of my left hand,
With the flaming noon
    to my right.

And at my feet,
    a swirling watery vortex
    into which I must leap.
I am given no time to prepare,
    and I must trust
        that my connections will hold.

The Guardians stand
    at the corners.
Each blessing me in turn
    with the substance of their beings.

Covered in white wings
    I step off into
        the Void.
The darkness has substance,
    and fills my eyes, my nostrils,
        my mouth.
I am packed in the stuff of darkness.

And I emerge into a haven
    with permission to rest.

The Guardians surround me
    in a circle dance
    of shifting symbols
    and archetypes.

Offering a pattern of
    connections.

IMMRAM

Immram
Voyage to the West.
Voyage to the Celtic Otherworld,
    to the Isles of the Blessed,
          the Land of Youth,
          the Land of Women,
          the Land of Promise,
          the Land Under the Wave.

We travel within our souls
    to a place better than this one,
        better than we can make.

We recognize our own tracks
    all over this place,
And long for a place,
    beyond our chaotic grasp,
Where those wiser than us
    wait with the answers.

That place where my questions
    will be answered.

Or, maybe,
    I won't need my questions.

Immram

AT THE WINTER DANCES

I watch the young men
    in their feathered finery.
They dance the eagle and the hawk,
    the deer and the ram.
Each step following the tracks,
Each foot set down in the
    Grand Pattern.

And the little boys,
    so carefully dressed and feathered,
    following their elders,
    learning the pattern.
Their eyes sparkle and dart
    like dragonflies.

The two buffalo dancers,
    mark the center of the pattern,
    vivid in their intensity.

At the center she dances,
    the one young woman.
Elegant presence,
    in her hand the sacred corn.

The chorus moves in front of me
    the line of drums filling the air.
I stand in the pulse
    and listen to the sky throbbing.

And I see the plaza from above,
    a spot of color and motion
        in the vast still stony hills.

Through eagle's eyes I see
    the village and the fields.

I look into the moistly fertile sky
    and see lightning jump
        from eagle's wings.

And feel all things connected,
    all my relations.

AT THE WINTER DANCES

MANANNAN, CELTIC SEA GOD

He reaches forward through the mists
    of shifting myth and paradigm,
An ancient name, surviving each wave
    in a new vessel.

Each layer of civilization
    defines and describes a single gateway,
    while chinking up the peepholes
    of its predecessors
            with newer and better explanations.

And yet, through the strata
    of stone, bronze, and iron,
        the ages of faith, reason, and information,
Come shards of pure light
    glinting through the shifting alignments.
Tantalizing slivers of ancient paradigm.

Manannan.

Those drawn to silent, ancient tongues
    and ink trails,
Ferret him out of myth and folk-tale.
They find him, mature and graceful,
    welcoming the bringers of wisdom.
One of the Old Ones,
    in the company of The Mother and The Good God.

Each tale, each watery clue,
    shows him to be the Landless One
            at home in the sea.
The waves his white horses,
    King of the Land Under the Waves.

He comes bearing a branch from Avalon,
    the Land of Apple Trees.
In fruit and flower at once,
    golden apples whose chimes gift
            a healing sleep.

Landless, yet he divides the land,
    giving the Middle World to
        our own kind,
    the Underworld to the Faerie Folk,
        the people of magic and mist,
            of the Sidhe,
        sending them into the fairy mounds.

And we, in our information age,
    alone among our kind,
Possess the gift of Pattern.

Two paths lie open.
    The work of chinking up the holes
        a "time-honored profession"
            not lacking enthusiasts.

Or we can lift the intricately woven screens
    from vellum and parchment,
        from song and tale
                from stitch and stroke,
    Align and shift them,
            hold them up to the sun,
            play with the patterns
    And watch for pinholes of light.
            Scan the starlike patterns,
                    read the light years,
            And discern the archetypal wisdom.

Manannan.

I take my brush into my hand and create,
            an impression.
    I stalk through myth and method
            looking for alignments.
I hold my glimpse of Manannan before me.

I look through his screen,
        taking along his Horses out of the Waves,
            and Trees of the Otherworld.
I place them around the fairy mound,
        and find myself leafing through books,
        looking at images.

The Irish sun disc
    rides the Danish stone-carved ship.
Different myths
    watch the sun rise
            out of the sea.

Looking at images of Newgrange.
    They say he gave this mound to faerie noblility,
            gave them three gifts,
                    concealing mists,
                    immortality, and freedom from want.

Yet the image which calls to me,
    is the carved stone at the back of the mound,
        kerbstone 52,
        the one whose markings
                seem to indicate an opening into the hill
                hidden from generations of
                persistent archaeologists.
        An opening as yet invisible
                to any worldly senses.

And the stone opening my brushes define,
    comes not from this hill,
    but from Dowth, across the valley.

The winter solstice sunset marks,
    at once,
    this stone
    and this passage.

The winter solstice sun,
    rises and enters
            the visible passage into Newgrange,
    passes over the mounds on its
            shortest journey of the year,
    and sets, sending the last thin winter beams
            across the face of kerb 52
                    and down the passage into Dowth.
    Dancing at each moment
            across stone-carved spirals
    which send me to photographs
            of a place nearer to my own time and place.

Photos of
    a shard of summer solstice light
            slipping through the layers
            of Chaco Canyon stone,
            dancing over a stone spiral.

And stitching together,
    human remnants.

Reminding us,
    that we are family,
            rooted together.

And we can
    understand each other.

MANANNAN, CELTIC SEA GOD

GRANDMOTHER SPIDERWOMAN

Out of the chaos
    She weaves order,
    Her knobby fingers
    walk the threads.

We all know her.
    She wears different names,
    But her fingers are always
        walking the threads.
            Spinning,
            Weaving,
            Knitting,
            Embroidering.

She combs fibers of Chaos
    into the patterns of Delight,
    inventing new colors and textures
    in her play.

We remember her lessons.
    We remember the time before,
    and when she taught us
    to use our hands and our minds
        for change,
        for Change.
    She gave us the gifts,
        the skills.
    We are clever students.

It is she who has separated us
    from the others.

Because of her we know the power
    of Big Change.
    We lean into our power
    and draw ourselves away
        from the others.

But our clumsy fingers
    are tearing the web.
    We are blind in our
        cleverness.

And if we listen closely,
    We can still hear her spinning,
    We can find the pattern,
        of Her stitches.

She gave us the gifts,
    And she waits for us to
    See the pattern,
    To be seduced by the beauty
        of the pattern,
    And to weave our own way
    Back into the Web.

GRANDMOTHER SPIDERWOM

THE ARTIST'S HANDS

My Hands,
    Two Birds Circling me,
    As I watch them perform
    From inside my skull.

They begin to play,
    And I bcome a watcher,
    Contentedly observing
    The birth going on before me.

And these birth waters
    Feed my roots,
    And feed the earth.

My Blood Rivers flow,
    Branching and meandering,
    Surging and Circling,
    Connecting the birds
        To the Puzzler, Playing
            Inside my skull.
        To the Deep Well Within,
            from which flow
            the free floating
            Particles of Meaning

The winter tree puts off all show,
    Sinks her roots deep into
        the Rich and Juicy, and,
    Cradles Spring.

THE ARTIST'S HAND